灯与夜蛾

Library and Archives Canada Cataloguing in Publication

Title: The lantern and the night moths : five modern and contemporary Chinese poets / selected and translated by Yilin Wang = Deng yu ye e / Wang Yilin.
Other titles: Deng yu ye e
Names: Wang, Yilin (Poet), translator.
Description: Chinese characters in title transliterated. | Poems in original Chinese and in English translation. Supplementary text in English.
Identifiers: Canadiana (print) 20230589235 | Canadiana (ebook) 20230589375
        ISBN 9781778430381 (softcover) | ISBN 9781778430398 (EPUB)
Subjects: LCSH: Chinese poetry—20th and 21st centuries—Translations into English.
        LCGFT: Poetry.
Classification: LCC PL2658.E3 L36 2024 | DDC 895.11/608—dc23

Edited by Khashayar Mohammadi and Chenxin Jiang
Cover art by Ciaoyin Luo | Interior design by Megan Fildes and Jasmine Gui
Typeset in Laurentian, with thanks to type designer Rod McDonald

Invisible Publishing is committed to protecting our natural environment. As part of our efforts, both the cover and interior of this book are printed on acid-free 100% post-consumer recycled fibres.

Printed and bound in Canada.

Invisible Publishing | Halifax, Fredericton, and Picton | www.invisiblepublishing.com

Published with the generous assistance of the Canada Council for the Arts, the Ontario Arts Council, and the Government of Canada.

THE LANTERN AND THE NIGHT MOTHS

灯与夜蛾

FIVE MODERN AND CONTEMPORARY CHINESE POETS

SELECTED AND TRANSLATED BY

YILIN WANG 王艺霖

Halifax | Fredericton | Picton

For my wàigōng and wàipó.

Thank you for sharing your love of poetry,

storytelling, and the written word.

献给我的外公外婆

感谢你们让我领略中文文学之美

Being an immigrant in the diaspora can often feel like drifting in a vast ocean with no shorelines in sight. When home isn't a person, or a place, or memories, but a wisp of smoke just beyond my grasp, a glass castle so ephemeral and elusive, poetry is one of my rare lifelines. It's the closest that I have ever felt to belonging.[*]

* Excerpted from Yilin Wang's personal essay, "Faded Poems and Intimate Connections: Ten Fragments on Writing and Translation" (first published as a part of the League of Canadian Poets' National Poetry Month blog series in 2022).

秋瑾
Qiu Jin

(1875–1907)

满江红·小住京华

小住京华，早又是、中秋佳节。
为篱下、黄花开遍，秋容如拭。
四面歌残终破楚，八年风味徒思浙。
苦将侬、强派作蛾眉，殊未屑！

身不得，男儿列；
心却比，男儿烈！
算平生肝胆，因人常热。
俗子胸襟谁识我？英雄末路当磨折。
莽红尘、何处觅知音？青衫湿！

A River of Crimson:[1] A Brief Stay in the Glorious Capital

A brief stay in the glorious Capital,
    and soon, it's Mid-Autumn Festival again.
Sheltering by the fence, chrysanthemums bloom everywhere;
    the autumn air cool and clear, as if freshly cleansed.
The folk ballads of conquered lands fade in all four directions
    as the kingdom falls ultimately in defeat;[2]
the aftertaste of these past eight years
    makes me long wistfully for Zhèjiāng.
Bitterly forced to behave as a wife with painted brows,
    I'm full of disdain!

Not a man in the flesh,
    unable to walk amongst them;
but the heart exceeds,
    more fierce than a man's!
I think of my strong spirit,
    stirring often with passion on others' behalf.
How can narrow, uncultivated minds
    comprehend my nature?
A hero at the path's end
    must suffer trials and tribulations.
In the crimson-dust world, where can I find my kindred spirit?
    My plain robe is stained with tears!

菩萨蛮·寄女伴

堪怜一片帘前月，不照欢娱照离别。云树思悠悠，无情湘水流。
一山相隔远，欲见何由见？含笔费商量，愁和更漏长。

寒风料峭侵窗户，垂帘懒向回廊步。月色入高楼，相思两处愁。
聊得心上事，托付浣花纸。若遇早梅开，一枝应寄来。

Púsāmán:[3] To a Female Friend

Take pity on the slice of moon beyond the curtains,
    shining not upon joyous gatherings, but rather, partings.

The wistful longings of clouds and trees extend on and on.
    The Xiāng River's currents flow, heartless and cold.

A mountain in between us, the distance so vast.
    When will we finally reunite as we yearn to?

Holding an ink brush between my teeth, I mull over words,
    fretting late into the night as the water clock drips on.

Cold gusts of wind pierce and invade windows.
    Drawing the curtains closed, I wander down the corridor.

Moonlight seeps into this tall pavilion.
    The melancholy of longing, here and elsewhere.

To converse on matters lingering within one's heart,
    imparted on the floral letter-papers of Huànhuā Brook.[4]

If you chance upon a plum blossom, flowering early
    amidst the snow, send a branch of it this way!

偶有所感用鱼玄机步光威哀三女子韵

妆台喜见仙才两，客路飘蓬月又三。
明镜萧疏青翼鬓，闲窗宽褪碧罗衫。
十联佳句抚膺折，一卷新诗信手衔。
道韫清芬怜作女，木兰豪侠未终男。
高吟白雪谁能继？欲步阳春我自惭。
小院伫闻莺睍睆，旧巢留待燕呢喃。
爱翻声谱常抛绣，为买图书每脱簪。
身后微名豹雾隐，眼前事业蚁沙含。
交游薄俗情都倦，世路辛酸味久谙。
绿蚁拼将花下醉，黄庭闲向静中参。
不逢同调嗟何益？得遇知音死亦甘。
怅望故乡隔烟水，红牙休唱忆江南。

Spontaneous Thoughts

with the rhyme from Yu Xuanji's poem that follows another
poem by the three sisters Guang, Wei, and Pou[5]

At the vanity table, I meet two waves of immortal talents with delight.
    On the travellers' road, adrift like weeds, till it's the third lunar month again.
In the clear mirror, my black hair like cicada wings, turning thin and dismal.
    Closing the window, I languish away as my jade-green gown loosens.

Ten couplets of fine verse, I read admiringly, with a hand over my heart.
    Another scroll of new poetry arrives, and I snatch it up quickly.
Daoyun, her character as pure as fragrance, sadly a woman.
    Mulan, a bold and free-spirited warrior, didn't remain a man.

Who can carry on singing the high, refined notes of "White Snow"?
    I blush with shame as I endeavour to render "Bright Spring."[6]
In the courtyard, lingering, the singsong of warblers.
    Old nests remain and await returning swallows' chirping.

To often abandon needlework for a love of rhyming dictionaries.
    To always strip off hair ornaments to pay for books.
For a humble reputation in the afterlife, the leopard retreats into the mist.
    In the undertakings ahead, there are pests that spew poisonous sand.

Socializing in frivolous ways exhausts all my sentiments.
    Long have I tasted pungent bitterness on the path of life.
Freshly brewed rice wine, savoured to the fullest, tipsy under blossoms.
    The Yellow Court Classic,[7] a leisurely search for wisdom amidst tranquility.

When no one else shares my tune, what is the point of sighing?
    To meet a kindred spirit who cherishes the same songs, I'd willingly die.
Sorrowfully I gaze towards my hometown, across misty waters.
    Sandalwood clappers should stop singing "Memories of Jiāngnán."

自题小照（男装）

俨然在望此何人？侠骨前生悔寄身。
过世形骸原是幻，未来景界却疑真。
相逢恨晚情应集，仰屋嗟时气益振。
他日见余旧时友，为言今已扫浮尘。

Inscription on My Tiny Portrait (in Men's Clothes)

Solemnly I gaze ahead—who is this before me?
  The bones of a vigilante–hero from a past life, resentful of this body.

The physical masculinity of a deceased self is mere illusion,
  but the envisioned future can become reality.

Regretting that we didn't know each other sooner, let us unite,
  heads held up high, sighing at the times, spirits emboldened.

In the future, when I meet my friends from bygone times,
  I shall declare, I have swept the dust of the world away.

日人石井君索和即用原韵

漫云女子不英雄，万里乘风独向东。
诗思一帆海空阔，梦魂三岛月玲珑。
铜驼已陷悲回首，汗马终惭未有功。
如许伤心家国恨，那堪客里度春风？

A Reply to Ishii-kun in Matching Rhyme

Don't speak so easily of how women can't become heroes—
  alone, I rode the winds eastward, for ten thousand miles.

My poetic ponderings soared, a lone sail across the vast, expansive sea,
  dreaming wistfully of the Three Islands,[8] exquisite under moonlight.

The imperial palace's bronze camels have fallen, the grief unbearable.
  The toiling warhorse is guilt-ridden, not one battle yet won.

As my heart weeps over my homeland's loathsome troubles,
  how can I linger, a guest abroad, savouring spring winds?

有怀
游日本时作

日月无光天地昏，沉沉女界有谁援？
钗环典质浮沧海，骨肉分离出玉门。
放足湔除千载毒，热心唤起百花魂。
可怜一幅鲛绡帕，半是血痕半泪痕！

Reflections
written during travels in Japan

Sun and moon without light. Sky and earth in darkness.
  Who can lift up this drowning world of women?

I pawned my jewels to sail across the endless deep-blue sea,
  torn from my offspring as I departed my homeland at Jade Gate Pass.[9]

Unbinding my feet to cleanse away a millennium's poisons,
  I awaken the spirits of women, hundreds of flowers, abloom.

Oh, this pitiful handkerchief made of merfolk-woven silk,
  half stained with blood and half soaked in tears!

Dear Qiu Jin: "To Meet a Kindred Spirit Who Cherishes the Same Songs"

Moonlight seeps into this tall pavilion.
  The melancholy of longing, here and elsewhere.

The autumn moon is a common motif within Chinese poetry, shining often upon geographies of homesickness and longing. In your poem, "Púsāmán: To a Female Friend," written over a hundred and twenty years ago, the moon casts its light on a different kind of yearning—the search for a zhīyīn 知音. Literally "the one who can truly understand your songs," a zhīyīn is a close friend, a kindred spirit, a queerplatonic soulmate who shares your deepest ideals. If I had lived in the same era as you, amidst the tumultuous sociopolitical changes of the late Qīng dynasty, the backdrop against which your feminist views emerged, might we have crossed paths and even become each other's zhīyīn?

But more than a century has passed since your death, and I live here in Vancouver, an ocean's distance away from your final resting place by the West Lake in Hángzhōu. The only thing I can do is to glance up at the moon that we still share, bright and wistful as ever. As I read and savour the melody of your words, I wait alone in this room for your voice to rise from among the pages, slowly, to cross time and distance, until it's as if we're sitting side by side, meeting for the first time, chatting spiritedly late into the night.

∿

To converse on matters lingering within one's heart,
  imparted on the floral letter-papers of Huànhuā Brook.

May I share the story of how I first encountered your work? I was searching for a new Chinese feminist poet to translate, in order to push back against the systemic, ongoing erasure of feminist writers within both Sinophone and Anglophone publishing, when a friend suggested, in a serendipitous yet perhaps also fated conversation, *what about Qiu Jin's poetry?* Of course I was familiar with your name, well aware of your reputation as a Chinese feminist revolutionary. But I had no idea that you were also a poet, let alone that in the thirty one years of your life, you left behind over two hundred poems, nearly all of which were only published posthumously.

Please translate Qiu Jin's words, the friend urged. Over the years, she had lovingly acquired a number of edited collections of your poetry, which were out of print and especially difficult to find in North America. Generously she offered to pass them along to me. And soon, a thick package holding three of your books arrived at my door. I accepted the package gently, and felt the weight of your words in my hands.

~

To often abandon needlework for a love of rhyming dictionaries.
  To always strip off hair ornaments to pay for books.

What was it like for you as a young woman growing up near the end of the Qīng dynasty? You were privileged enough to be born into a literati-official's family, able to access books that most girls could only dream of, yet still expected to write only about "feminine" topics, in the subtle and reserved styles befitting "proper etiquette."

It's clear from even your earliest poems, however, that you rebelled fiercely against the traditions of women's poetry, in particular the "guīyuàn" 闺怨 genre, which the scholar Yan Haiping has eloquently translated as "boudoir sorrows."[10] The genre always features a female speaker, her voice full of melancholy, rendered passive by the dual "boudoir" of cloistered chambers and gender roles. Unable to visit a male lover or husband who is far away, she pines, endlessly, through day and night.

Did you realize, as I also did while reading classical guīyuàn poetry, that despite its supposed focus on women's sorrows, it was actually popularized by many male poets of the Táng dynasty (including Li Bai 李白, Du Fu 杜甫, and others), who co-opted the female speaker's struggles for their own purposes? Her pain about the lack of male attention became a mirror for the male author's frustrations about the lack of imperial favour. Her bitterness about a man's absence served as a way for him to offer thinly veiled critiques of wars in the borderlands.

Pushing against the fraught history and conventions of this genre and against a society where a woman's life was often defined by her patrilineal ties and by heteronormative expectations of marriage, your poems reclaim the voice, body, and heartache of the woman in the boudoir. She transforms into a rebel. A free-spirited poet who casts aside needlework to flip through books. A daring heroine who travels far beyond the confines of her home to pursue her own ambitions. Repeatedly she expresses her longings on her own terms, not for romantic love, but for a zhīyīn.

～

Solemnly I gaze ahead—who is this before me?
The bones of a vigilante–hero from a past life, resentful of this body.

As you broke through and shattered the "boudoir sorrows" tradition, you turned instead to writing poems that evoke a long lineage of cross-dressing heroines from history, such as Hua Mulan, Mu Guiying, or Qin Liangyu. When I translated your poem "Inscription on My Tiny Portrait (in Men's Clothes)," I found myself asking what it would be like to inhabit your body. The poem was inscribed on the back of a photo that showed you cross-dressing in a traditional gown commonly worn by men in the late Qīng dynasty. You posed sternly, unsmiling, as you stared straight into the camera.[11]

When you wrote this poem, how did it feel to carry the bones of a past self within you? When you expressed your resentment towards your body, were you describing what's now commonly known as dysphoria? As you imagined your past and future selves meeting, did you find solace in the collapse of that binary and in the gender fluidity that emerged? As a genderqueer femme, I find strength in your poems about gender and cross-dressing, and I wish that I could join you in sweeping the world's troubles away.

〜

Sun and moon without light. Sky and earth in darkness.
  Who can lift up this drowning world of women?

More than a century after you died in a failed uprising against the Qīng government, your name now appears frequently in history books, and you are held up as a celebrated revolutionary. But when I ask other Sino diaspora poets, literary translators, and graduates from Chinese literature programs if they have read your poetry, whether in Chinese or in translation, the majority of them tell me that no, they have not. This answer comes as no surprise. Many literary history textbooks in China still gloss over your poetic contributions, especially the works touching on feminism, gender inequality, and cross-dressing. While some of your poems have been translated into English by Sinologists, their translations are nearly always intended for an academic readership. Instead, I approach your work as a queer femme and poet–translator of the diaspora.

I can almost hear you sighing with frustration as I explain that the poetry written by racialized writers of marginalized genders—that's to say, cis and trans women, trans men, nonbinary folks, and anyone who is questioning—are *triply* underrepresented in English translation, simultaneously along the axes of language, race, and gender. Only roughly three percent of the books published in the United States each year are translations into English, a phenomenon that has been dubbed the "Three Percent Problem."[12] Furthermore, the vast majority of the works chosen for translation are written by white Europeans. And out of all the English translations of Sinophone poetry books published from 2008–2022, only twenty-six percent are written by women poets and twenty-six percent translated by women translators (based on data gathered by *Publishers Weekly*'s Translation Database, which unfortunately only records gender identity in a binary and incomplete way).[13]

～

When no one else shares my tune, what is the point of sighing?
  To meet a kindred spirit who cherishes the same songs, I'd willingly die.

Late on a Saturday night, the moon was once again shining brightly outside my window as I translated your poetry. I took a break to browse the web, and stumbled across a Facebook post about your work being featured in the British Museum's "China's Hidden Century" exhibition. Intrigued, I investigated further, and was shocked to discover images and videos that showed the exhibition was using my previously published translations of your poetry, including the complete text of "A River of Crimson: A Brief Stay in the Glorious Capital." The museum had never contacted me for permission, yet had been using my translations prominently in multiple formats in their ticketed exhibition for over a month, without credit or compensation. I was utterly stunned.

Years ago, I began translating your poetry with the hopes that it could help your work reach a wider Anglophone audience, so you would have more zhīyīn. Now I was caught in a long, exhausting, and seemingly endless public battle to defend our words, both your poetry and my translations. To ensure that they were not displayed insensitively, with incorrect line breaks, or erased from the exhibition entirely, but treated with the respect they deserve as works of art. As the anniversary of your death came and passed on July 15, I couldn't help but dwell on the fact that I was now the same age as you were when you courageously took a stand and died for your beliefs. I longed to bring a bouquet of chrysanthemums, your favourite flowers, to your gravesite by the West Lake. All I could do, however, was keep speaking out for both of us.

It took nearly two months before a settlement was finally reached. I had to fight against gaslighting and microaggressions, and even fundraise for legal fees. Eventually, your poetry and my translations were restored to the exhibition, this time with permission, reasonable pay, and proper credit. The long overdue resolution wouldn't have been possible without the help of countless people and communities—racialized folks, fellow writers, editors, translators, readers, academics, museum professionals, asexual and aromantic organizers, and even members of the BTS Army—all of whom rallied to spread the word about the incident and supported us along the way. Articles about our work appeared not only in Anglophone news outlets, but also in Chinese (both Simplified and Traditional), Japanese, Indonesian, French, Italian, Spanish, and German, each an acknowledgement that we had been heard, at long last.

All these voices of encouragement are still with me now as I return to translating your poetry. As the melody of your words rises again from the pages of second-hand books graciously gifted by my friend, I feel as though I'm no longer chatting with someone whom I had just met, but rather a collaborator who I had fought many battles alongside. A long-lost zhīyīn, the one with whom I share the same songs. I hope that your spirit can rest more easily now and in the days to come. Although you might not have met many kindred spirits who truly understood you in your own lifetime, your poetry has now touched new readers in various corners of the world.

---

1   A River of Crimson 满江红 is a cípái 词牌 (poetic form).

2   In the source text, these two lines contain an idiom that alludes to the defeat of the Chǔ Kingdom 楚国 during the Hàn dynasty 汉朝.

3   Púsāmán 菩萨蛮 is a cípái 词牌 (poetic form).

4   In ancient China, writers and scholars often wrote letters on special types of hand-crafted letter writing paper. The female poet Xue Tao 薛涛, who lived during the Táng dynasty, invented a popular and highly prized type of paper known as "Huànhuā Brook-style paper" 浣花笺, which was so named because she made it using the water from Huànhuā Brook.

5   While the source poem's title mentions a rhyme scheme, this is not present in my translation. Rhyme in Mandarin is much subtler, and also, the pronunciations of Mandarin words have changed significantly since centuries ago, so many texts that once rhymed no longer do.

6   *The Book of Chu* 《楚辞》 contains a story of a minstrel whose performance of a popular and simple song was initially accompanied by thousands of audience members. But as she performed more technically and stylistically advanced songs, fewer and fewer folks could follow along. By the time she reached the songs "Bright Spring" and "White Snow," almost no one could keep up. These two songs thus came to stand for artistic creations that are so highly sophisticated and full of artistry that they are only able to be appreciated by a select few.

7   *The Yellow Court Classic* is a Daoist text.

8   Multiple annotated editions of Qiu Jin's poetry, including 《秋瑾全集笺注》 and 《漫云女子不英雄: 秋瑾诗词注评》, state that this is an archaic name for Japan.

9   The Jade Gate Pass 玉门关 is a fortified pass along the Great Wall located to the west of Dūnhuáng in modern-day Gānsù province. It was known in ancient times for being at the edge of the kingdom, specifically as the final Chinese outpost for travellers on the Silk Road. The pass has since then become widely used as a stand-in for the border.

10   Yan Haiping, "Qiu Jin and Her Imaginary," in *Chinese Women Writers and the Feminist Imagination, 1905–1948* (London: Routledge, 2006), 33–36.

11   The photo, originally from *Qiū Jǐn yánjiū zīliào: wénxiàn jí* 秋瑾研究资料:文献集 (Research Materials on Qiu Jin), eds. Guo Changhai 郭长海, Qiu Jingwu 秋经武, et al. (Yínchuān 银川: Níngxià rénmín chūbǎnshè 宁夏人民出版社, 2007), is reprinted in Hu Ying, "Figure 3.06," *Burying Autumn* (Cambridge: Harvard University Asia Center, 2016), 151–2.

12   "About," Three Percent, The University of Rochester, accessed July 30, 2023, http://www.rochester.edu/College/translation/threepercent/about/.

13   "Translation Database," *Publishers Weekly*, accessed Oct 16, 2023, https://www.publishersweekly.com/pw/translation/home/index.html. Copyright (c) PWxyz LLC, Publishers Weekly. Used with permission.

To calculate the percentage of translated Chinese poetry books published from 2008–2022 that were originally written by women poets, I searched the database with the following search criteria: the publication years set as "2008–2022", the source language as "Chinese," the genre as "poetry," and the author's gender as "female." This returned twenty-one entries. I then repeated the search with the same criteria, but with the author's gender left unspecified, which returned a total of eighty-two entries. Dividing twenty-one by eighty-two gave me a number that rounds up to twenty-six percent. I then repeated a similar search process for the gender of translators and calculated the corresponding percentage for women translators.

张巧慧
Zhang Qiaohui

(1978–)

方言

回老家帮母亲搬花草
月季、玉树、吊兰、铜钱草
全都搬到屋外过夜
母亲说它们需要背背露水

仿佛露水降临时
它们全都伏身向下
仿佛露水也是神的一部分

听母亲说——面朝黄土背朝天
母亲种地时，也像一株植物
母亲说方言时，又像一个土地神

Dialect

Returning to my hometown, I help Mother carry her potted plants
the China roses, jade succulents, hanging spider plants, and pennyworts
all need to be brought outside to spend the night
Mother says, *their backs need to bask in some dew*

As if in the moment that the dew drops descend
the plants will all bend over and lean down
As if each dew drop is also a trace of a deity

Listening to Mother repeat the saying——
to labour facing the yellow earth, with your back to the sky
When she toils in the fields, she too is like a plant
When she speaks in dialect, she's also like a deity of the land

千秋塔

异乡之夜，彼岸有塔
通体的光安慰了我，
神总会在黑暗中现身，于高处
看护着红尘

早上我看清塔的真相
现代仿古建筑，钢筋混凝土和砖结构
它的平凡安慰了我
活在人间，我们需要朴素的认同
一个华侨把思乡之情立在高处
告诉游子
故土是神
又像无用的装饰

The Pagoda of a Thousand Autumns

On a night far from home, I glimpse a Buddhist pagoda on the other shore
It comforts me with its body full of light
A deity shall always appear in the darkest hours, towering from up high
to watch over the crimson-dust world of mortals

Next morning, I perceive the true face of the pagoda
a pseudo-classical reconstruction made of bricks and reinforced concrete
It comforts me with its mundanity
As we drift through society, we crave acceptance, plain and simple
A member of the Sino diaspora placed their homesickness in a spot up high
to impart to the wandering traveller:
the ancestral land is a deity
and also, a useless decoration

独白

你知晓祖母葬于何处，却不知道
祖母的祖母在何处

教场山上的坟墓早已迁走，草木葳蕤
在人间，有个短语叫死无葬身之地

——我在遗址上，等待更多碎片呈现

他说四十过后的女人最为无情
她不为风月所动
他爱恋的那个二十岁的女人善于抒情
她羡慕一座坟以及坟前盛开的桃花

盛开，是喧嚣的集体自尽
而死亡，是独白

——站在拆迁的墓地前
我忽然想起桃花坞的姑娘，
我还等着青草从水泥地里长出来

Soliloquy

You know where Grandma is buried, but do not know
where Grandma's Grandma is

Jiàochăng Hill's graves have long been displaced, now covered by lush greenery
In the mortal world, a saying, *to be without a resting place even after death*

   I stand at the former burial ground, waiting for more fragments to surface

He claimed a woman over forty was the most heartless
She wasn't moved by the romance of the moon and winds
The twenty-year-old woman he loved was so lyrical
She idealized the grave and the peach blossoms blooming before it

To be in full bloom is a boisterous act of collective suicide
Whereas, to die, is a soliloquy

   Standing before the demolished graveyard,
   I suddenly recall the young lady among the blossoms
   I am still waiting, for spring grass to sprout from concrete

天一阁

斑驳的碑刻与修补残书的人
完成对时光的注解
天一阁的下午
有蝉鸣，鱼钻出水面，几片树叶落下
有快递员匆匆取出包裹
这是新的，也是旧的
——这鲜活的、生动的，
名叫短暂。莲花盛开，
也叫短暂。有人在廊下打盹
醒来已是黄昏
——而你起身，向那久长而盛大的
致敬。你这样描述：
万物短暂，却因看到而获得重生
物是人非，却因书籍而获得永恒

你于藏书楼下消磨半日，没翻一本书
风过，却到处是翻书的声音

Tiānyī Gé, the First Library Under the Sky[1]

Stone carvings mottled with age and restorers of damaged books
are working to complete annotations on the fleeting light of time
At Tiānyī Gé in the afternoon
cicadas sing, fish poke their heads out of ponds, a few leaves cascade
The delivery person hands out packages hurriedly
These are the new, and also, the time-worn——

the vibrant and the lively
are known as the ephemeral. A lotus flower in full bloom,
also called an ephemeral. Someone naps under a covered walkway
and by the time they awaken, it will already be dusk——

Yet you rise now to pay homage to
that which is majestic and long-lasting. You state:
The world's ten thousand beings are all ephemeral,
    but through being perceived they'll become born anew
Everything has changed and shall keep on changing,
    but through books the fleeting will be preserved for eternity

For half a day, you idle away by the Bibliotheca, and never open a single book
The wind stops, and still, everywhere, the rustle of pages turning

举着鞭子的手停不下来

要收集多少偏方才能治愈我的病
这个偏执的女人，敏感于一方残碑，
却对满坡的春花无动于衷。

而她曾是助产士，亲手触摸过生
后来她写诗，写泡椒凤爪、棉胎被絮、过境台风
还有猝逝的友人、中元节、孤魂
仅有一首写到工作，写一个外地女人
难产而死。窗外，有人在玩陀螺
我脸颊发烫，那鞭子，在抽
我央她写写接生的事吧，
胎动、呼吸，新鲜的生
一个女人怎样帮助另一个女人分娩……
人间最美的刑罚，母亲和死神，各司其职

"是的，一开始就伴随着撕裂、疼痛与哭喊
以及冷眼旁观的死神。"
"但还有比死亡更美的事"

窗外，有人在玩陀螺。
那举着鞭子的手停不下来

The Raised Hand with the Whip Won't Stop

How many folk remedies will it take to finally cure my illness?
This unrelenting woman is so attentive to a fragmented stele,
yet so indifferent to all the spring blooms that cover the hillside.

And she used to be a maternity nurse, caressed birth with her hands
Later, she wrote poetry about chicken feet with pickled peppers,
duvets and comforters, the typhoons passing through
wrote about departed friends, the Ghost Festival, lonely spirits
Only a single poem about work, an out-of-town woman
dying from obstructed labour. Outside the window, someone is spinning a top[2]
My cheeks burn; the whip keeps whipping
me, pleading to her, *oh, write about the delivery of newborns*,
fetal movement, breathing, the tender newness of birth
how one woman helps another with the parturition——
The most exquisite trial of the mortal world,
the Mother and the God of Death, each carrying out their role

"Yes, it begins with a ripping apart, harrowing pain, and tearful cries
with the God of Death staring coldly from the sidelines."
"But there's something even more beautiful than death"

Outside the window, someone is spinning a top.
The raised hand with the whip won't stop

废墟

精神的废墟。哲学的废墟。文化的废墟。
坟墓，是人的废墟
照片，是光阴的废墟；记忆，是思念的废墟
语言是你的废墟。你是秩序的废墟
晚饭是日子的废墟，垃圾桶是生活的废墟
我是女儿的废墟
……我被废墟包围。掐断的牵牛花又开出一朵
浅蓝色的花。浅蓝色，是疼痛的废墟

Remnants

The broken shambles of the spirit. The crumbling ruins of philosophy.
    The vestiges of culture.
The grave is the lingering remains of a human being
Photos, the faded imprints of fleeting light and shadows;
    reminiscence, the residue of longings
Language is the remnant of you. You are the debris of social order
Dinnertimes are the scraps of passing days,
    trash cans the junkyards of life unfolding
I am the rundown, decrepit home of my daughter
——Ruins surround me on all sides. Wounded by pruning,
the morning glory blooms anew
with a light-blue flower. The light blue, a dwindling trace of tender pain

On Zhang Qiaohui: Translation as Diasporic Yearnings

方言 | Dialect

For over twenty years I have lived in the Sino diaspora. The vast majority of my waking hours are now spent thinking, speaking, and writing in English. Translating Sinophone poetry, however, has become the most meaningful way in which I have been able to maintain a deep connection with my mother tongues. Not only do I rely on my knowledge of written Chinese—which I acquired through my formal and informal education in Mandarin—to parse every ideograph of a poem, but I also read the lines aloud to hear their cadences in Mandarin and Sichuanese. To reference a Chinese dialect is always to evoke a linguistic tie to a particular place, for Sinophone dialects can be as distinct as languages, differing by region, province, city, and even village or neighbourhood, so specific that they can denote exactly where someone is from. Qiaohui doesn't name the dialect that she speaks. To savour the rhythm of her poetry in the Yíbīn branch of the Sìchuān dialect of my ancestral hometown, which I inherited from my grandparents, is therefore a powerful act of intimacy. As I translate Qiaohui's poetry, I linger in the language of home, kinship ties, and ancestral lands. I imagine her words anew, for all of us in the diaspora who share complex or fraught relationships with our mother tongues.

千秋塔 | The Pagoda of a Thousand Autumns

When I feel uprooted and directionless, I often turn to Sinophone poetry for solace, just as the wanderer in Qiaohui's poem searches for a Buddhist pagoda in the misty darkness. As the speaker insightfully observes, those of us residing far away from a distant home can have a tendency to romanticize it. But I am not seeking to physically return to the pagodas that overlook my hometown. Rather, I believe that the *yearning* for home is, in itself, a language of diaspora. When I carry Sinophone poetry into English, I reconstruct a pristine replica of the pagoda that has long faded into the horizon for many and that has never been seen by others. It is built of simple words and hard labour. It's down-to-earth, unmagical, and merely decorative. It's a north star that glows steadfastly in the distance for those who need its reassuring light.

独白 | Soliloquy

You know where Grandma is buried, but do not know / where Grandma's Grandma is. So much family history and cultural knowledge can be hidden and lost as a result of displacement, immigration, and intergenerational trauma. My wàipó, the first woman in her family to attend school and become literate, was also the one who re-taught seven-year-old me how to speak Mandarin and Sichuanese after I had completely forgotten the languages as a result of spending three years overseas. Her teachings allowed me to become the translator I am today. The last time I saw her, she had been drafting a memoir, a book she vowed to share on my next trip home. But then she passed away before I could visit again, and her manuscript was nowhere to be found, no matter how desperately I searched. It's my longing for her lost words, and for all the stories that I'll never be able to read, about her mother, grandmother, and great-grandmother, which now drives me to fill the gaps they left behind. To seek out the voices of women poets from the past and present. To translate works that have been erased and forgotten.

天一阁 | Tiānyī Gé, the First Library Under the Sky

One of the most famous folktales about Tiānyī Gé, China's oldest surviving private library, features a young woman named Qian Xiuyun 钱绣芸, who longed for nothing more than to read the books inside Tiānyī Gé. Living during the reign of the emperor Jiaqing 嘉庆 (1796–1820), when women had little freedom, Xiuyun begged her parents and matchmaker to arrange for her to marry into the family that owned the library. But soon after her wedding, she discovered the misogynistic rules that forbid women from entering Tiānyī Gé, and she passed away in sorrow. Reincarnating as a rue plant, an herb known to protect books from insects, she was then finally plucked and carried into the library of her dreams. When I turn to face my shelves of Chinese poetry books, I often recall this tale and the afternoon that I spent in 2018 wandering through Tiānyī Gé's grounds. I read, write, and translate poetry for women like Xiuyun. Her life was so fleeting, but her story has been preserved through the written word. It shall remain in the minds of those who truly perceive and understand her.

举着鞭子的手停不下来 | The Raised Hand with the Whip Won't Stop

Storytellers often compare the writing process to pregnancy and childbirth. As a poet–translator, I feel much more akin to a nurse who helps a poem to reincarnate and enter its next life. Like the nurse in Qiaohui's poetry who turns away from the fields of blooming flowers to dedicate all her efforts to a fragmented stele, I also step around the latest, bestselling, and most renowned Sinophone literary works to seek out poetry that has been overlooked. How does one go about bringing a literary text, so tender with warmth, vulnerabilities, and lyricism, into a distant, unfamiliar world that it might not be ready to encounter? I must guide it with gentle hands to ensure its spirit is kept alive and intact during this transformative, and often excruciating process. So much care and sensitivity are required to ensure a poem survives as it is reborn into a new language, screaming, kicking, and crying.

废墟 | Remnants

A poem, or its translation, is a legacy deposited by the person who penned it, a careful arrangement of language that will one day outlive its creator. Likewise, a poet–translator of the diaspora is also a survivor; they have persisted against and even defied a publishing ecosystem with structural biases, rules, and hierarchies. When I face the page, surrounded by my many attempts to translate the word "废墟," which has no perfect equivalent in English, I feel as if I were trying desperately to cultivate a morning glory that was growing from a pile of rubble and debris. Meticulously, I embrace the task of pruning the plant, cultivating the inexpressible until it begins to multiply into words like "remnants," "residue," and "reminiscence." Each and every iteration bears testimony to that which has been lost, and even more importantly, all that courageously endures. As the struggles subside, a newly translated poem emerges, blooming once more.

---

1 Tiānyī Gé 天一阁, the oldest surviving private library in China, was founded in Níngbō in 1561. The name "tiānyī," literally "the first under the sky," is an allusion to the four-character idiom 天一生水 (tiān yī shēng shuǐ), which means "the first thing to emerge in the world was water." A "gé" is a type of ancient multi-storied building.

2 A "tuóluó," commonly translated as a "top," or a "spinning top," is a cone-shaped toy with a round body and a sharp tip at the bottom. It is made to spin by the force of a whip; the harder you whip, the faster the tuóluó will spin.

废名
Fei Ming

(1901–1967)

灯

深夜读书
释手一本老子道德经之后，
若抛却吉凶悔吝
相晤一室。
太疏远莫若拈花一笑了，
有鱼之与水，
猫不捕鱼，
又记起去年夕夜里地席上看见一只小耗子走路，
夜贩的叫卖声又做了宇宙的言语，
又想起一个年轻人的诗句
鱼乃水之花。
灯光好像写了一首诗，
他寂寞我不读他。
我笑曰，我敬重你的光明。
我的灯又叫我听街上敲梆人。

lantern

reading late at night
i set aside my copy of laozi's *dào dé jīng*,[1]
as if i have tossed away the auspicious and regrettable outcomes in life[2]
to meet face to face within this room.
so distant from when the buddha held up a flower quietly
and mahākāśyapa smiled back in silent understanding,[3]
there's the fish and the water they swim in,
the cat that doesn't catch fish,
then i recall the small rat that strode across the rug last new year's eve,
the night peddler's hawking has also become the universe's language,
then i remember another line of poetry by a youth
the fish is actually the water in full bloom.
the lantern light seems to have written a poem;
they feel lonesome since i won't read them.
i say with a grin, i revere your brightness.
my lantern then replies, listen
the night watch is striking a bamboo cylinder to mark time.

飞尘

不是想说着空山灵雨，
也不是想着虚谷足音，
又是一翻意中糟粕，
依然是宇宙的尘土，——
檐外一声麻雀叫唤，
是的，诗稿请纸灰飞扬了。
虚空是一点爱惜的深心。
宇宙是一颗不损坏的飞尘。

the floating dust of the mortal realm

not to speak of timely and wondrous rain falling upon ephemeral mountains,
nor to dwell on rare and unexpected footsteps echoing through nebulous valleys,
here's yet another predictable batch of grainy residue,
still the mortal dust of the vast universe, —
beyond the eaves, the lone call of a sparrow.
yes, pages of poetry, please become ashes and take flight.
the nebulous, ephemeral world is a speck of the deeply cherishing heart.
the universe is a particle of indestructible dust floating in the air.

出门

我走在街上，
心里惊讶着一个人类的记录，
这就是说诗人的诗，——
迎面来了一个朋友我不认识了，
这时我举目无亲，
百事皆非，
车水马龙
肩摩踵接
也正好不是一个空白，
我仿佛只有这个空白的是最能懂得的了。

to wander out

i'm strolling along the street,
my heart astonished by a record of humankind,
so this is poetry that speaks to how a poet is, ——
here comes a friend heading straight towards me, oh a stranger;
in this moment, i'm so far away from my home and loved ones,
everything has gone astray,
crowds and traffic sweep by in rushing waves
shoulders rubbing heels bumping
do not leave just one trace of emptiness,
it seems that this emptiness is the only thing i understand best after all.

掐花

我学一个摘花高处赌身轻
跑到桃花源岸攀手掐一瓣花儿，
于是我把它一口饮了。
我害怕我将是一个仙人，
大概就跳在水里淹死了。
明月出来吊我，
我欣喜我还是一个凡人
此水不现尸首，
一天好月照澈一溪哀意。

nipping flowers

like a youth betting on their nimbleness as they leap and snatch
    flowers from up high
i sprint to the otherworldly peach-blossom-shore[4] and climb up
    and nip a flower petal,
then swallow it in one giant gulp.
oh no! am i doomed to ascend and become a daoist–immortal?
better jump into the water and drown myself instead.
the bright moon rises, hanging in mourning
i'm delighted to see that i'm still a human being
these waters refuse to display any corpses.[5]
the day's fine moonlight illuminates the lamenting creek.

星

满天的星
颗颗说是永远的春花。
东墙上海棠花影
簇簇说是永远的秋月。
清晨醒来是冬夜梦中的事了。
昨夜夜半的星，
清洁真如明丽的网，
疏而不失，
春花秋月也都是的，
子非鱼安知鱼。

stars

the sky full of stars
each spark professing to be a spring flower that will bloom forever.

the shadows of begonias on the eastern wall
each spray claiming to be an autumn moon that will glow for eternity.

awakening in the early morning, all but a winter night's dream.

the midnight stars of yesterday,
pure and true, like a bright net overseeing the world,
sparsely woven yet ever infallible.[6]

the passing spring flowers and autumn moons are like this too—
the proverbial fish, unknowable to you who are not fish.[7]

On Fei Ming: To Translate Nothing and Everything

Writing from the 1920s to the 1940s, Feng Wenbing 冯文炳, better known by his pen name Fei Ming, penned a small yet influential body of work, roughly one hundred poems, that has earned him a reputation as one of China's most enigmatic poets. This is especially remarkable given that the Mandarin language already allows for ample ambiguity, because it does not contain verb tense conjugations, definite and indefinite articles, and distinctions between singular and plural nouns. Fei Ming's poetry, however, is ambiguous on a far deeper level.

I close read his poem "lantern" over fifty times during my dozens of attempts to translate it. Even as I admired the misty, often elusive beauty of his lines, I also became equally frustrated by all the ambiguous moments that resist easy interpretation. How are all the disparate references and images in the poem—the *Dao De Jing*, the *I Ching* divinations, the silent smile shared by the Buddha and Mahākāśyapa, the fish, the water, the cat, the rat, and the night peddler's hawking—connected with one another, if at all? When the speaker meets "face to face" within the room, with whom or what is the speaker meeting, since the grammatical object of the sentence is mysteriously unspecified? And how do all these moments link back to the lantern that appears in the poem's title and also "seems to have written a poem"?

As the weeks and months went by, I continued making tweaks, hoping in desperation that perhaps, by simply reading the poem one more time, I'd finally be able to coax it into revealing its secrets.

∽

Eventually, exasperated by my lack of progress, I contacted Thomas DeZauche, a religious studies professor with a specialization in Buddhism, Hinduism, and Sanskrit, hoping that he could shed light on the significance of the spiritual allusions in Fei Ming's poetry. Patiently, DeZauche explained Fei Ming's references, with a particular focus on the "Flower Sermon," which tells the story of how the Buddha held up a flower and Mahākāśyapa smiled back in immediate understanding.

The tale teaches us that not all knowledge can be expressed through language or verbal communication, DeZauche emphasized. Sometimes, wisdom cannot be taught, but only acquired through first-hand experiences. It needs to be emotionally felt. Intuitively gleaned.

Immediately, the fog of confusion inside me cleared. Just as the Buddha and Mahākāśyapa smiled at each other in quiet understanding, without the need for conversation, the poem "lantern" is also full of the unsaid and the inexpressible. During my many persistent and even obsessive attempts to "understand" Fei Ming's poetry, I had forgotten that a poem is so much more than the words on a page—it's also the gaps that the poet has left behind. The expansive space that lingers in between and around Fei Ming's words is here for readers to dwell in and reflect upon rather than explain away. Poems that appear enigmatic at first glance might be communicating in quieter and subtler ways, seeking to be experienced and felt rather than to be unpacked and rationalized. Isn't the art of translating poetry also the art of translating these silences?

～

But how exactly do you carry the idea of "postive emptiness" into a new target language where the concept tends to have negative associations? I face this exact challenge when translating the words "空" and "虚" in the poem "the floating dust of the mortal realm."

"空" means "empty" in certain contexts, but it's also the Chinese character chosen to represent the Buddhist concept of "śūnyatā."

Rather than having connotations of "nothingness," "absence," or "lack," "空" is spacious and airy, a poignant observation about the unfixed, unpredictable, and fleeting nature of the world. Eventually, I settle on rendering "空" as "ephemeral." The character "虚" holds similar connotations, but is associated with Daoism rather than Buddhism. It describes a state of constant flux, between the existent and the non-existent, between the fully present and the completely absent. Again, words such as "fragmented," "faint," and "illusory" are too negative, burdened with implications of inadequacy or false-hood. After much thought, I choose the word "nebulous" to represent the nuanced in-betweenness of "虚." In both cases, the parallel concepts of "空" and "虚," along with my translations, subvert conventional views of "blank spaces" as inherently lacking, and instead, illustrate all their complex, layered possibilities.

~

To better understand Fei Ming's love of the elusive and the unsaid, I delved into his theoretical writings on poetry. His preference for opacity was especially unusual given that he was writing during and after the New Culture Movement, a progressive movement that lasted from 1915 to the 1920s and that attempted to modernize the landscape of Chinese literature.

Inspired by the essays and poetry of Hu Shi 胡适,[8] a writer, poet, and intellectual at the forefront of this movement, many poets in the Sinosphere moved gradually away from writing verses in Literary Chinese 文言文, a formal written language with archaic diction and grammar, commonly thought to have been created during the War-ring States period (476–221 BCE) and taught only to the literati in the dynasties that followed. Instead, the writers of the New Culture Movement adopted Vernacular Chinese 白话, a colloquial written language with modern diction and grammar that closely resembles spoken Mandarin.

This modernization in language led to the emergence of a crucial question: in what ways should the new poetry written in Vernacular Chinese—known literally as "New Poetry" 新诗—be similar to or different from the long lineage of "Classical Poetry" 古诗, the formal poetry written in Literary Chinese, that precedes it? Into this discourse stepped many poets and literary theorists of the era. Among them was Fei Ming.

~

Some of Fei Ming's contemporaries, such as Hu Shi, advocated for a plain-spoken, naturalistic, and prosaic way of writing New Poetry, corresponding strongly to the colloquial nature of Vernacular Chinese. When Hu Shi criticized the work of Li Shangyin 李商隐 and Wen Tingyun 温庭筠, two poets from the late Táng dynasty (836–907 CE), for being indecipherable, Fei Ming responded by showering these poets with praise.

To insist on rationally deciphering the meaning of Li's cryptic poem "The Exquisite Zither" 《锦瑟》 is to miss the point entirely, Fei Ming argued. Instead, he expressed his appreciation for the elegant aesthetics of Li's poetry.[9] Dismissing the issue of clarity, he applauded Li and Wen for their strong sense of imagination, which, as the scholar Luo Xiaofeng 罗小凤 has insightfully noted, is demonstrated through techniques such as long strings of disconnected allusions, free association, and the use of dreams as a framing device.[10] I believe it is precisely these poets' vivid imaginations that have imbued their works with a misty, surreal, and elusive quality, which can be seen in Fei Ming's work as well.

~

Within the vividly imaginative poems of the late Táng dynasty poets, Fei Ming found a new "感觉,"[11] varyingly translated as feeling, mood, vibe, atmosphere, or sensibility. He advocated that these poets' writings should not be considered a "regression" from the particular standards set by their widely celebrated predecessors (such as Li Bai, Du Fu, and Wang Wei 王维), whose works have often been thought to collectively form the "golden age" of Táng dynasty poetry. Rather, he praised the late Táng poets for boldly deviating from the voices before them.[12]

Inspired by their spirit of rebellion and risk-taking, Fei Ming urged his own contemporaries who were experimenting with New Poetry to continue engaging with figurative language and devices that are commonly found within Classical Poetry, not by merely replicating them, but by subverting them in surprising ways. When crafting a poem centered on the motif of the autumn moon, for example, each poet ought to describe it in a startlingly new light, filtered through their own distinctive worldviews, aesthetics, and concerns as an individual living in the modern age.[13] Fei Ming followed his own advice well; his later poems placed popular references, such as the utopic Peach Blossom Spring 桃花源 or the proverbial fish in Zhuangzi's allegories 子非鱼，安知鱼之乐, in contexts utterly different from the original, reimagining them anew.

～

It is remarkable and even uncanny that the works of two late Táng poets, who lived around 1,200 years ago, seems to share many stylistic similarities with modernist poetry in English, especially in their embrace of the imaginative, experimental, and enigmatic. The same can likewise be said of Fei Ming's work.

It must be emphasized, however, that unlike his peers who turned away from classical literature to seek inspiration from Western poets and literary theory, Fei Ming's reading journey followed the opposite trajectory. His theoretical writings on New Poetry rose primarily out of his immersion in Sinophone rather than European classics, even though he was clearly acquainted with both. As his mentor Zhou Zuoren 周作人 recounted in the essay "In Memory of Fei Ming," Fei Ming "read Shakespeare and Harding while studying at Běijīng University," where he majored in English literature. He soon turned away from those works, however, and returned to "Du Fu, Li Shangyin, The Classics of Poetry, Confucius' Analects, Laozi, Zhuangzi, and eventually, Buddhist scriptures [...] then went down an even more esoteric and inexplicable path."[14]

～

I believe it is precisely Fei Ming's passion for the innovative and the avant-garde that has allowed his poetry to remain so timely and time-less even in the twenty-first century. His body of work is akin to an "ars poetica," a meta-reflection on the emergence of modern Sino-phone poetry. His poems have challenged me greatly as a translator, pushing me to observe and embrace the ambiguous, to seek out new ways of rendering the wondrous gaps and silences in his writing. His works contain numerous, complex, and at times contradictory layers of meaning—literal words, connotations, allusions, subversions, and especially, the ever inexplicable—which together have forced me to confront the impossibility of translating everything.

In the days to come, when I return to working with Fei Ming's words once more, I will greet the page with a question, not for it this time, but for myself. How will I bring my own touch to my trans-lations and *transform* Fei Ming's poems, just as his own writings shed new light on the power of the elusive and its importance to the progression of Sinophone poetry movements? Difficult choices and interpretations must be made when I am translating, but what is translation if not the gentle, rigorous art of embracing and pushing back against the constraints of language, in order to unsettle and to remake?

---

1   *Dào Dé Jīng* 《道德经》 by Laozi 老子 is often translated as *The Classic of the Way and Virtue*.

2   In the source text, this line refers to four types of possible outcomes that appear when reading fortunes based on the *Yi Jīng* 《易经》 (*The Book of Changes*): 吉 (good fortune), 凶 (calamity), 悔 (regret), and 吝 (remorse).

3   An allusion to the Buddha's "Flower Sermon."

4   This is a possible reference to Tao Yuanming's *Peach Blossom Spring* or the garden of immortal peaches that belongs to the Queen Mother of the West 西王母.

5   In Fei Ming's essay "Zhuāngtái jí qítā" 《妆台及其他》("The Vanity" and Other Poems), from *Féng Wénbǐng yánjiū zīliào* 冯文炳研究资料 (Research Materials on Feng Wenbing), he noted that he wrote this poem while reading a version of the Vimalakīrti Sutra annotated by the Chinese Buddhist philosopher Sengzhao 僧肇, who quotes Kumārajīva's words "海有五德。一澄净, 不受死尸。"

6   This line and the previous line are an allusion to the quote "天网恢恢，疏而不 失" from *Dào Dé Jīng* by Laozi.

7   This line is an allusion to the quote "子非鱼，安知鱼之乐？" from *Autumn Floods* 《秋水》 by Zhuangzi.

8   Susan Chan Egan, "Hu Shi and His Experiments," in *A New Literary History of Modern China,* ed. David Der-wei Wang (Cambridge: Harvard University Press, 2017), 242–48.

9   Feng Wenbing 冯文炳, "Yǐwǎng de shīwén yǔ xīnshī" 《已往的诗文学与新 诗》(The Poetry of the Past and New Poetry), in *Féng Wénbǐng yánjiū zīliào* 冯 文炳研究资料 (Research Materials on Feng Wenbing), ed. Chen Zhenguo 陈振国 (Fúzhōu 福州: Hǎixiá wényì chūbǎnshè 海峡文艺出版社, 1990), 150–60.

10   Luo Xiaofeng 罗小凤, "Feì Míng duì gǔdiǎnshī chuántǒng zhōng 'xiǎng xiàng' de zàifāxiàn" 废名对古典诗传统中 "想象" 的再发现 (Fei Ming's Rediscovery of the "Imagination" in the Classical Poetry Tradition), in *Chángshā lǐgōng dàxué xuébào (Shèhuì kēxué bǎn)* 长沙理工大学学报 (社会科学版) no.4 (July 2015): 87–95. https://www.cnki.net/KCMS/detail/detail.aspx?d-bcode=CJFD&dbname=CJFDLAST2015&filename=CSSC201504014&unip-latform=OVERSEA&v=_cSwhx9s4LB28egf44pyV3zikjQVAir4DYBKkwTgIH-N5OJ23eXI3zP6F_GYoQAoB

Luo Xiaofeng 罗小凤, "Shī de gǎnjué yǔ xiǎngxiàng—1930 niándài Feì Míng duì gǔdiǎnshī chuántǒng de zàifāxiàn" 诗的感觉与想象—1930 年代废 名对古典诗传统的再发现 (The Emotions and the Imagination in Poetry: Fei Ming's Rediscovery of the Classical Poetry Tradition in the 1930s), in *Hǎinán shīfàn dàxué xuébào (Shèhuì kēxué bǎn)* 海南师范大学学报 (社 会科学版) no.8 (August 2016): 47–54. https://www.cnki.net/KCMS/de-tail/detail.aspx?dbcode=CJFD&dbname=CJFDLAST2016&filename=HL-SY201608009&uniplatform=OVERSEA&v=15I82S7LZKSte4gJQt3QEZ-8zuY2U_q7ggyz4B3A3f7aSl3njsM2df7fCqXFYRfeK

11   Feng Wenbing 冯文炳, "Xīnshī wèndá" 新诗问答 (Q&A on New Poetry), in *Féng Wénbǐng yánjiū zīliào* 冯文炳研究资料 (Research Materials on Feng Wenbing), ed. Chen Zhenguo 陈振国 (Fúzhōu 福州: Hǎixiá wényì chūbǎnshè 海峡文艺出版社, 1990), 135–40.

12 Feng Wenbing 冯文炳, "Xīnshī yīnggāi shì zìyóushī" 新诗应该是自由诗 (New Poetry Should Be Free Verse) in *Féng Wénbǐng yánjiū zīliào* 冯文炳研究资料 (Research Materials on Feng Wenbing), ed. Chen Zhenguo 陈振国 (Fúzhōu 福州: Hǎixiá wényì chūbǎnshè 海峡文艺出版社, 1990), 141–49.

13 Feng Wenbing 冯文炳, "Xīnshī wèndá" 新诗问答 (Q&A on New Poetry), in *Féng Wénbǐng yánjiū zīliào* 冯文炳研究资料 (Research Materials on Feng Wenbing), ed. Chen Zhenguo 陈振国 (Fúzhōu 福州: Hǎixiá wényì chūbǎnshè 海峡文艺出版社, 1990), 135–40.

14 Zhou Zuoren 周作人, "Huái Fèi Míng" 怀废名 (In Memory of Fei Ming), in *Féng Wénbǐng yánjiū zīliào* 冯文炳研究资料 (Research Materials on Feng Wenbing), ed. Chen Zhenguo 陈振国 (Fúzhōu 福州: Hǎixiá wényì chūbǎnshè 海峡文艺出版社, 1990), 58.

小西
Xiao Xi

(1974-)

关于树的无数可能

一棵树
有时是门，有时是床
有时是刀柄和菜板，弹弓和陀螺
有时是箱子，或者扁担

有时是一把琴，弹破了江山
有时是无数铁锹，掩埋了真相

有时是两个醒来的纸人
抬着棺木
去往天堂的路上，遇到了火

the infinite possibilities of trees

a single tree
sometimes, it's a door; sometimes, a bed
sometimes, a knife handle and a cutting board, a slingshot and a spinning top
sometimes, a storage box, or a carrying pole

sometimes, a lone qín,[1] its chords shattering the kingdom's rivers and mountains
sometimes, endless shovels, burying the truth

sometimes, two just-awoken people made of paper
shouldering a wooden coffin
on their way to heaven, they encounter bright flames

倒车，请注意

注意身后的石头，小草
雷鸣与闪电。
注意奔跑的孩子和猫
老人以及安静的树。

注意腐烂的果实
刚刚落下的雪。
注意车轮下的蚂蚁
碎玻璃反射出来的光。
注意滚动的皮球
不怀好意的钉子。
注意霾中那张悲伤的脸
丢了盖子的陷阱。

注意讨钱的手。
注意蹦在地上未响的炮仗。
注意路边突然失控的哭声。

the car is backing up, please pay attention

be mindful of the rocks behind you, the tiny blades of grass
the roars of thunder, and the flashes of lightning.
watch out for the sprinting kids and cats
for the elderly and the hushed trees.

take note of the rotten fruits
of the snow freshly fallen.
look out for the ants under your car tires
the light reflected on broken glass.
be on guard about rolling leather balls
nails with malicious intentions.
behold the sorrowful face in the mist
the traps that have lost their lids.

pay attention to the hands begging for money.
beware of firecrackers on the ground that haven't yet gone off.
take heed of the sudden, uncontrolled sobs from the roadside.

卖针

有人卖楼，卖车，卖酒肉
她在卖缝衣针。
有人卖毒，卖肾，卖青春
她在卖缝衣针。

她慢腾腾地摆着
每一包大小号齐全
每一根都无比尖锐

我想蹲下来问问：过去能不能补
人心能不能补
这个世界快得漏洞百出，有没有办法补

selling sewing needles

some people advertise dream homes,
promote luxury cars,
peddle sumptuous wines and meats

she's selling sewing needles.

some people deal illicit drugs,
auction their kidneys off to pay for iPhones[2]
exploit the springtime of their youth to strike it rich

she's selling sewing needles.

she lays them out slowly, without hurry
each pack complete with all the sizes large and small
each needle incredibly sharp and pointed

i want to squat down and ask: can the past be mended
can human hearts be mended
this world moves so quickly, rupturing with hundreds of holes,
is there a way to mend it?

另一种语言

有时感觉语言受到了限制
石头不能滚落到山下
樱树，斜在峭壁上

我的祖辈，都是农民
他们被犁伤害
又离不开土地

火车呼啸而至
弄出很大的动静
不过是按着既定的轨迹

还是看看海水吧
它填满了虚空
就要溢出时，又迅速撤回

而凤头鸊鷉，海鸥和船
是另一种语言
浮在深蓝的水面上

a different kind of language

sometimes, there's a feeling that language has been restricted
tumbling boulders cannot reach the foot of the mountain
the cherry tree grows, slanted on the steep cliff face

my ancestors, all of them were farmers
they were deeply wounded by the blades of the plough
yet also utterly reliant on and inseparable from the land

a train whistles loudly as it arrives
making a grand, dramatic entrance
but it's merely following its predestined tracks

let's go instead to seek the waters of the sea
it fills the vast, empty void
until it's nearly overflowing, then swiftly withdraws

while the great crested grebes, seagulls, and boats
form a different kind of language
adrift on the deep azure sea

风不止

舔着糖纸的孩子，糖块掉入泥中。
腊梅下唱西厢记的，多是孤独老人。

投掷到湖里的石子，已回到岸边。
凋谢的花，重上枝头。

帐篷漏雨，不是雨的错误。
瓜果腐烂，亦非天气意愿。

请风退到风中，闪电藏于袖内。
爱回到爱里，小指勾住小指。

当钟表停止了摆动
修理时间的人，正在路上

the ceaseless wind

a child licks the candy wrapper, their treat fallen into the mud.
those who sing *romance of west chamber* under wintersweet trees, mostly
   lonely elders.

the stones cast into lakes, all of them have returned to shore.
the flowers that wilted, abloom from the tips of branches once more.

tents leak during storms, it's not the fault of the rain.
fruits spoil and rot, it's not the will of the weather.

please let wind return to the wind's midst, let lightning hide in the sleeves.
love returns to the act of loving, two pinkies hooked onto one another.

when the hands of clocks are no longer moving
the repairer of time is already on their way here

命运和诗意

在简陋的路边店里
有人正向一碗白米饭致敬。
秋天了
但他颗粒无收，行囊是空的。
他的胡茬高于地里收割后的庄稼
饥饿令他的手颤抖，嘴唇急切地
贴近瓷碗。

湖里的残荷卷起裙摆
稿纸被风吹到地上。
此时，我正和朋友通话
说好了，对命运和诗意
大家不再妥协。
当我起身离开时，看见他正蹲在地上
捡起掉落的米粒，小心地放进嘴里。

between life's hardships and poetic beauty

in a hole-in-the-wall restaurant overlooking the road
there's a man paying his tributes to a bowl of white rice.
it's autumn already
but he hasn't reaped a single grain, his travel sack empty.
his long thick beard is more plentiful than the harvest from the field
hunger makes his hands tremble, and his lips move eagerly
toward the porcelain bowl.

in the lake, the shrivelled yet tenacious remnant of a lotus leaf curls up its skirts
manuscript pages scatter in the wind and fall onto the floor.
in this moment, i'm on the phone with a friend
promising each other that, when it comes to life's hardships and poetic beauty
we shall not compromise anymore.
when i rise to leave, i spot the man squatting low
picking up a fallen grain of rice, placing it into his mouth with utmost care.

On Xiao Xi: The Infinite Possibilities of Poetry Translation

"诗的魅力就是在于它给了读者想象力的最大空间，它好像说尽了什么，又好像永远无法说尽。"

"The power of poetry is that it gives readers the utmost space to imagine. Poetry seems to speak of everything, yet never can it say it all."

— 小西 Xiao Xi[3]

关于树的无数可能 | the infinite possibilities of trees

Although a tree is easily overlooked as a common part of many people's everyday surroundings, it has the potential to transform into things far more powerful than we might first imagine. Likewise, even the most ordinary words within a poem, often taken for granted within the source language, can correspond to a myriad of options in the target language, which I must carefully consider before making a difficult yet necessary choice. Let me recount my process for translating the word "无数" to illustrate. The word that comes first to mind is "countless," a close literal translation. But is this word, with its focus on counting, the most suitable one for describing all the things that a tree could become, its numerous possibilities? There's also "limitless," though the word is associated more with human potential than with nature. "Endless"? This translation feels closer, but it shifts the focus to how a tree's potential is everlasting and eternal. I continue searching for another word that better conveys, emotionally and tonally, not the endless potential of a tree, but rather the incredible number of things that it could become. This leads me, eventually, to choose the word "infinite," which encapsulates a tree's incredible ability to transform and also, fittingly, the power of literary translation.

倒车，请注意 | the car is backing up, please pay attention

But not every word has a perfect equivalent in another language, even if you sift through all the possibilities. "注意," for example, has a meaning close to "pay attention to." A crucial difference lingers, however: "注意" is universally applicable to every scenario, whereas in English, verbs and action phrases tend to be much more situationally specific, as shown by the examples, "watch out for the sprinting kids and cats," "behold the sorrowful face in the mist," and "beware of firecrackers on the ground."

The challenge of translating "注意" into English, difficult enough in one instance, is compounded by the fact that the word appears ten times in the original poem, in the title and at the beginning of each and every line. This intense repetition results in a wonderfully rhythmic, emotional build-up in the source text, but would feel repetitive and even monotonous if replicated directly in English. Giving up on finding one perfect match for the word "注意," I decide instead to translate it gradually, over the course of the entire poem. I guide readers through many iterations of the word, line by line, until the variations accumulate over time, to emphasize not just the importance of paying careful attention— to both the world around us and to language—but also, the many, varied ways in which we can look, observe, and behold.

卖针 | selling sewing needles

Still, there are moments when the meaning of a word cannot be fully expressed in one single translation, nor through a series of translation attempts. Sometimes, Xiao Xi's poetry uses diction that evokes nuanced sociopolitical connotations, allowing her to offer sharp, insightful commentary on contemporary Chinese society. A "毒" is a poison or toxin, but to sell a "毒" is to deal hard drugs in a nation where many people continue to experience the intergenerational trauma that resulted from the Opium War. A "肾" is a kidney, but to sell a "肾" is to follow a few misguided people obsessed with luxury, who longed so desperately for the newest iPhone that they sold their most vital organs on the black market to acquire one. "青春" is youthfulness, but to sell "青春" is to deliberately pursue lines of work that rely heavily on one's good looks, fit body, and youthful energy—such as modelling, serving, or acting—in a race against time to accumulate wealth, with full awareness of the overt and intense ageism and sexism that still dominate most workplaces. It is very difficult to convey all of these connotations attached to the poem's diction by translating the words on the page alone. I turn instead to the technique of glossing. By adding brief descriptors to many of the nouns, I hint, even if only subtly, at their sociopolitical contexts, hoping that this can encourage readers to reflect more deeply about the issues that Xiao Xi's poem comments on.

另一种语言 | a different kind of language

But what do I do when there is so much historical, cultural, and sociopolitical context or baggage that even the skillful use of descriptive glosses cannot adequately convey all the layers of implied meaning? The phrase "离不开土地," which literally means "inseparable from the soil and the earth," is an example of this scenario.

On the surface, the line refers to the fact that many Chinese people living in the countryside have long been or are still farmers, completely dependent on their land for survival, food, and basic needs. But the ties that people share with the earth run far deeper than this. It lingers in the ancient myth of how the goddess Nuwa sculpted humans out of clay. In how an individual's sense of self and belonging is often closely linked to their ancestral home-town and home province. In the long-held belief that the body of the deceased must be laid to rest properly in the earth for them to obtain peace in the afterlife. In the sociopolitical movements of the twentieth century (like the Land Reform Movement) that reshaped the lives of millions. In present-day government policies that restrict people's migration and access to social benefits based on the municipality in which they were born or reside.

To translate all this information would be excessive and feel overwhelming, requiring lengthy explanations far beyond what Xiao Xi has written. I decide simply to add one word—*utterly*—to modify the phrase "reliant on and inseparable from the land." I can only trust that this will be enough to emphasize the depth of people's ties to the earth and to invite readers to consider their own relationships with the land they live on.

风不止 | the ceaseless wind

In addition to translating moments where words or phrases carry a lot of implied context, I also sometimes face the opposite challenge, where I must find ways to render ambiguous and elusive phrases and ideas in English. Verb conjugations do not exist in Manda-rin, so markers of time and hypothesis, often taken for granted in Anglophone writing, are frequently absent from the poems that I translate. The title of the poem "风不止" highlights this issue. Is it that the wind hasn't stopped? The wind won't stop? The wind can't stop? The wind doesn't stop? The wind isn't stopping? The wind would not stop? The wind will not stop? Or the wind will never, ever stop? After considering all these possible interpretations, I end up sidestepping the uncertainty altogether, moving away from the question of time to focus on the wind's actual movement, and ren-dering the title as "the ceaseless wind."

This ambiguous representation of time also appears in the last two lines of the same poem. Did the hands of clocks fall to a stop in the past, or are they only stopping now, right in this moment? Had the repairer of time already been on their way to fix the clocks when the clocks started breaking down, or is the repairer only heading out now, in the aftermath? Again, I try to sidestep these questions, using phrases like "are no longer moving" and "already on their way here," to intentionally inhabit the grey area between past and present. I hope my decision to preserve ambiguities in Xiao Xi's poetry can encourage all of us to reconsider default assumptions about the need for certainty, both in translations and in our conceptual understandings of time.

命运与诗意 | between life's hardships and poetic beauty

A translator isn't merely a translator of words, but also of connotations, contexts, and implied meanings. Sometimes, they even carry entire worldviews across vast linguistic and cultural divides. The idea of "命运," for instance, is typically rendered as "destiny" or "fate." "Destiny" feels very dramatic and epic, as if someone is waiting in the wings to step into a particular role that they have long been destined for. "Fate" is more uncertain and mysterious, like someone glancing into the cloudy future, wondering what fate will inevitably befall them.

Yet the "命运" referred to in this poem is a grittier concept, reflected in the gesture of a man who picks up a fallen grain of rice and drops it carefully into his mouth. His act of desperation reflects people's struggles with limiting life circumstances, especially those that are pre-determined from the moment of their birth and that are difficult to overcome. "诗意," in contrast, is much more idealized, referring not only to the meaning of poetry, but also its romanticized, lyrical quality, which I have rendered as "poetic beauty." The speaker of this poem seems to struggle with "life's hardships" while aspiring to hold onto "poetic beauty," even though they no longer wish to compromise. As a poet–translator, I must also work with many limitations—like the linguistic constraints of Mandarin and English and the specific details of the source texts—but I nevertheless strive to challenge those boundaries in pursuit of my poetic ideals. And I invite you, readers, to join me in appreciating the powerful possibilities that this act of boundary-pushing can offer. Let us open our collective imaginations to other languages, literatures, and worlds.

---

1   A seven-stringed zither-like Chinese instrument.

2   This is an allusion to some widely reported incidents in China when people with limited income sold their kidneys on the black market in order to afford luxury goods like iPhones.

3   "Xiǎo Xī: shīgē, búzài yuǎnfāng érshì rìcháng" 小西: 诗歌, 不在远方而是日常 (Xiao Xi: Poetry is not in the distance but in the everyday), *Qīngdǎo Ribàoshè* 青岛日报社 (Qingdao Daily Press). November 24, 2022 https://epaper. qingdaonews.com/qdzb/html/2022-11/24/content_18903_7012835.htm (accessed Aug 1, 2023).

戴望舒
Dai Wangshu

(1905–1950)

戴望舒

我思想

我思想，故我是蝴蝶……
万年后小花的轻呼
透过无梦无醒的云雾，
来振撼我斑斓的彩翼。

I Think

I think, therefore I am a butterfly…[1]
Ten thousand years later, the gentle call of a tiny flower
shall travel through misty clouds that know nothing of dreams or awakenings,
to stir and shake my bright, iridescent wings.

古意答客问

孤心逐浮云之炫烨的卷舒，
惯看青空的眼喜侵阈的青芜。
你问我的欢乐何在？
——窗头明月枕边书。

侵晨看岚踯躅于山巅，
入夜听风琐语于花间。
你问我的灵魂安息于何处？
——看那袅绕地，袅绕地升上去的炊烟。

渴饮露，饥餐英；
鹿守我的梦，鸟祝我的醒。
你问我可有人间世的挂虑？
——听那消沉下去的百代之过客的跫音。

To Answer the Visitor with Classical Imagery

The solitary heart chases the splendid unfurling of wandering clouds.
The eyes, so familiar with cerulean skies, delight in the encroaching weeds.
Where does my happiness dwell, you ask?
    Upon the bright moon beyond the window, and within the books by my bedside.

When dawn arrives, watch the mist meander above mountain peaks.
As night descends, listen to the winds chatter amidst fields of flowers.
Where does my spirit linger to rest, you ask?
    Look at the wisps of cooking smoke above chimneys, curling slowly as they rise.

Sip dew when parched; dine on petals when hungry.
The deer watches over my dreams; birds greet my awakenings.
Am I burdened by the cares and concerns of the human world, you ask?
    Harken to the fading footsteps of the hundreds of generations passing by.

赠克木

我不懂别人为什么给那些星辰
取一些它们不需要的名称，
它们闲游在太空，无牵无挂，
不了解我们，也不求闻达。

记着天狼，海王，大熊……这一大堆。
还有它们的成份，它们的方位，
你绞干了脑汁，涨破了头，
弄了一辈子，还是个未知的宇宙。

星来星去，宇宙运行，
春秋代序，人死人生，
太阳无量数，太空无限大，
我们只是倏忽渺小的夏虫井蛙。

不痴不聋，不做阿家翁，
为人之大道全在懵懂，
最好不求甚解，单是望望，
看天，看星，看月，看太阳。

也看山，看水，看云，看风，
看春夏秋冬之不同，
还看人世的痴愚，人世的倥偬，
静默地看着，乐在其中。

For Jin Kemu[2]

I don't understand why some people feel the urge
to give unnecessary names to celestial objects.
They wander leisurely in outer space, free and unattached,
not comprehending us, nor seeking to win fame.

To remember Sirius, Neptune, Ursa Major—so many of them,
along with their compositions, their bearings,
you have racked your brain, made your head explode,
toiled away for a lifetime, but the universe remains unknowable.

Planets come and go, the universe carries on still,
spring passes and autumn follows, humans die and are born.
The suns endless in number, the outer space infinitely vast.
We're tiny and fleeting, summer insects, frogs at the bottom of wells.

To gloss over the mistakes of youth is the way of the elder.
To overlook rather than scrutinize is the wiser path of being.
Do not seek to understand it all, but rather merely to observe.
Gaze at the sky, the stars, the moon, the sun.

Also gaze at the mountains, the rivers, the clouds, the winds,
at the differences between the four seasons.
Gaze too at the human world's foolishness, its never-ending toils;
observe quietly without speaking, find joy in the act.

戴望舒

乐在其中，乐在空与时以外，
我和欢乐都超越过一切的境界，
自己成一个宇宙，有它的日月星，
来供你钻究，让你皓首穷经。

或是我将变成一颗奇异的彗星，
在太空中欲止即止，欲行即行，
让人算不出轨迹，瞧不透道理，
然后把太阳敲成碎火，把地球撞成泥。

To be joyfully immersed, outside the bounds of space and time.
Joy and I will transcend beyond all the realms,
become a universe of our own, with its sun, moons, and stars,
waiting for you to explore, deep into your white-haired old age.

Or I shall become a strange and peculiar comet,
pausing in space as I please, and travelling as I please,
so no one can calculate my trajectory, or see through my logic.
Then I shall shatter the sun into broken fire, smash planet Earth into mud.

秋夜思

谁家动刀尺？
心也需要秋衣。

听铰人的召唤，
听木叶的呼息！
风从每一条脉络进来，
窃听心的枯裂之音。

诗人云：心即是琴。
谁听过那古旧的阳春白雪？
为真知的死者的慰藉，
有人已将它悬在树梢，
为天籁之凭托——
但曾一度谛听的飘逝之音。

而断裂的吴丝蜀桐
仅使人从弦柱间思忆华年。

Autumn Night Reflections

Who is sewing with needle and thread?
The heart also needs autumn clothes.

Heed the tearful beckoning of weaving merfolk,
heed the breath of falling tree leaves!
Wind seeps into every vein and artery,
eavesdropping on the heart as it withers and breaks.

A poet once stated: the heart is a qín.
Who else knows the archaic songs,
"Bright Spring" and "White Snow"?
For the solace of the true connoisseur and kindred spirit who has died,
someone has hung it from the tip of a tree branch,
to lift up the ethereal melody—
the once carefully savoured, and now, departed tune.

Yet the refined instruments of Wú strings and Shǔ wood have shattered,
leaving only echoes of chords, reminiscent of those splendid years.

夜蛾

绕着蜡烛的圆光，
夜蛾作可怜的循环舞，
这些众香国的谪仙不想起
已死的虫，未死的叶。

说这是小睡中的亲人，
飞越关山，飞越云树，
来慰藉我们的不幸，
或者是怀念我们的死者，
被记忆所逼，离开了寂寂的夜台来。

我却明白它们就是我自己，
因为它们用彩色的大绒翅
遮覆住我的影子，
让它留在幽暗里。
这只是为了一念，不是梦，
就像那一天我化成凤。

Night Moths

Circling the halo of candlelight,
night moths dance in wretched repetition.
These banished spirits from Buddha's kingdom do not think about
the insects already dead, the leaves yet to die.

Moths are said to be napping kinfolk,
soaring across the steep mountains and passes of distant borderlands,
soaring across the far-apart longings of clouds and trees,
to soothe us in our misfortunes,
or else the dead ones who miss us,
pulled by memories, returning from the hushed netherworld.

But I see myself in the moths,
for their vast colourful silken wings
have overtaken my shadow,
abandoned it in grave darkness.
All for a single conviction, not a fantasy,
but that day I transformed into a phoenix.

On Dai Wangshu: Poetry is What Survives Translation

Dai Wangshu was not one of the most celebrated and renowned Chinese poets of his generation, but also one of the most prolific poetry translators working from the 1920s to the 1940s, translating literature from French, Spanish, Italian, and Russian into Mandarin. Sometimes, when I speak with non-translators about poetry translation, I hear them repeat the common myth that "poetry is untranslatable." In these moments, I recall how Dai debunked this misguided view in his essay, "Brief Fragments on Poetic Theory."[3] He argued passionately that as long as a poem is not solely reliant on the superficial flaunting of wordplay, it ought to always be translatable into other languages, unhindered by challenges such as linguistic differences, geographic distance, or even the passing of time. (Naturally, he wasn't referring to malicious translations that intentionally distorted the meaning of the original texts, he further clarified.) Dai's unwavering faith in the translatability of poetry has offered me much comfort as a poet–translator working in the present day. I can almost imagine him reaching out from decades past to whisper, grinning as he reassured me, "Don't worry, poetry isn't what is lost in translation, but rather, what survives it."

≈

It is especially meaningful for me that Dai's motives for pursuing translation align so closely with my own. In the afterword of his translation of Charles Baudelaire's *Les Fleurs du mal*,[4] Dai explained that translating Baudelaire's work was meaningful for him in two main ways. Firstly, he wanted to see how the qualities of Baudelaire's writing might be preserved or changed when carried into Mandarin. Secondly, he hoped that his translations would allow more Chinese readers to access the work of this unique yet under-translated French poet. Likewise, ever since I first began translating Sinophone poetry, I have been driven by a deep desire to share the work of poets I long admired, especially voices that are often underrepresented in translation. By experimenting with recreating their work in English, I hope to expand existing understandings of Sinophone poetry in the Anglosphere. The aspirations that Dai and I share remind me that as I translate his work, I am also continuing the task that he began nearly a century ago, almost as though I am just picking up right where he left off.

~

Many of Dai's poems explore the relationship between the self and an other, whether a butterfly, night moths, or people such as friends, travellers, and ancestors. In the poem "I Think," the line "I think, therefore I am a butterfly" combines an allusion to Zhuangzi's "Butterfly Dream" parable with René Descartes's philosophical statement "I think, therefore I am." In the original parable, Zhuangzi had a dream in which he became a butterfly, and then woke up, confused about who he was. Was he the Zhuangzi who had dreamed about transforming into a butterfly, or was he in fact a butterfly, having a dream about being Zhuangzi? The merging of this allusion with Decartes's marks a further breakdown of the boundary between the speaker and the butterfly, between dreaming and awakening, between Eastern and Western philosophies. It is a wonderful encapsulation of how deeply intertwined Dai's various influences are, how the works he was exposed to as a poet and translator were clearly always informing one another, inseparable. Indeed, as Dai's close friend Shi Zhecun 施蛰存 wrote in the preface of *The Poetry Translations of Dai Wangshu*, the three main periods in Dai's career as a poet paralleled his interest in translating the works of various French Symbolist, French Neo-Symbolist, and Spanish anti-fascist poets, respectively.[5] There is no doubt that my translations of Sinophone poetry, a practice also rooted in close reading, shall enrich my own writing as well.

Dai's passion for translation led him to prioritize it even during his many travels. In a series of dated journal entries collectively entitled "Diaries from a Sea Voyage,"[6] Dai wrote frequently about dedicating time to labour over his translations while on a month-long journey from China to France, where he was heading to study abroad. He traversed languages at the same time that he ventured across land and sea, wandering through bustling coastal cities for the first time, all while carrying bittersweet feelings of homesickness. His astute observations of the ports he passed through, the alluring cityscapes he beheld, and the stimulating conversations he shared with fellow travellers must have all enriched the translations that he was working on, making his practice feel truly lived-in and embodied in comparison to the act of working in isolation. Dai's approach to translation has inspired me to try my best to immerse myself in the world that he inhabited and let that inform my own translations. Listening to popular Chinese jazz songs from the 1930s and 1940s, I pore over his words, working from coffee shops full of vintage decor. Gazing at the pedestrians passing by outside, I try to imagine myself following his footsteps, wandering leisurely through the cobblestone streets of Paris.

In Dai's poem "To Answer the Visitor with Classical Imagery," the speaker replies that their happiness rests "within the books by [their] bedside." It is not surprising then that many of Dai's essays documented in remarkable detail his knowledge of book stalls, shops, and markets in many neighbourhoods of Hong Kong (where he resided for around seven years),[7] Paris (where he studied abroad),[8] and Madrid (where he visited during his travels in Europe).[9] Meticulously, he noted each bookseller's specializations, the discounts they offered, and the quality of books sold. These visits no doubt informed his knowledge of both established and emerging voices in the source literatures he worked with. They also attest to his love of books as material objects to be scouted for, bargained over, and carefully cherished. Living in the Sino diaspora—where Sinophone books, especially the newest releases and rare out-of-print editions, are often difficult to come by—I resonate strongly with Dai's urge to keep careful track of all the ways that he could access books written in the languages he translated from. It was no easy feat to build the small yet growing collection of Chinese books I now own. The volumes came from small independent bookstores and ethnic grocery stores hidden in Chinatowns and Asian malls scattered across Metro Vancouver. From sales held by other diaspora folks parting with their beloved collections. From cargo ships that travelled across the ocean for weeks and months on slow voyages, carrying long-awaited parcels. From kind friends who sacrificed their precious carry-on space to lug books back from overseas.

～

The many years that Dai spent living abroad also gave him the chance to meet in person with and befriend some of the poets who penned the works that he translated. In his essay, "On the Poet Supervielle," Dai recalled that on his last day in Paris, he decided to pay a visit to Jules Supervielle,[10] whom he met for the very first time just before departing the city. They enjoyed a pleasant stroll together in the mellow rain as they exchanged praise about each other's poetry. Before they parted, Dai asked Supervielle to handpick some favourite poems from his own body of work for Dai to translate into Mandarin. Dai could have easily made this request through writing a letter, yet he decided to visit in person to obtain Supervielle's permission and paid special attention to Supervielle's own preferences. This thoughtful gesture demonstrated how much respect Dai held not only for the works he translated, but also for the poets he worked with. Sadly, unlike Dai, I have not yet been able to meet in person with any of the Chinese poets I collaborate with. We live countless miles apart, but thanks to the help of text messaging applications, we can still hold long, extended conversations about our favourite verses and about the joys and challenges of the writing life.

As we consider Dai's dedication to the work of translation and how prominent a role it played in many aspects of his life, I also want to emphasize that he was not alone in his endeavours, but a part of a larger movement—a generation of poet–translators who worked in the aftermath of the New Culture Movement of the 1910s and 1920s. As poets embraced the transition from Literary Chinese to Vernacular Chinese—and some, like Fei Ming, boldly re-envisioned what modern poetry could look like by revisiting the classics— there was also an explosion of interest in Western and European literary theory, criticism, and philosophy, all of which made their way into Mandarin through an influx of translations. In the afterword of *A Centennial Anthology of Essays on the Translation of Chinese and Western Poetry*,[11] the editor Hai An 海岸 wrote that during the 1920s and 1930s, many poet-translators like Guo Moruo 郭沫若, Wen Yiduo 闻一多, and Xu Zhimo 徐志摩 all took on the crucial tasks of translating poetry and engaging in discourses about translation theory. Their translation practices not only inspired their own writings and greatly influenced the development of modern Sinophone poetry, but also left a lasting impact on the generations that followed, including many of China's contemporary poets.

Despite living in that remarkable era when literary translation truly flourished in the Sinosphere and was highly regarded by writers and scholars alike, Dai still felt that translated poetry was being severely overlooked by the publishing industry, which he criticized in his essay, "Discussions on the Translation of *Cyrano*."[12] I'm saddened by the fact that so many decades later, little seems to have changed, at least not in mainstream Sinophone and Anglophone publishing spaces—although many poet–translators continue to work from the margins, as persistent as ever.

As I follow the path of Dai and others like him, I cannot help but recall his poem, "Night Moths." While moths are traditionally seen as the spirits of deceased ancestors returning home, the speaker of the poem sees themself in the moths as well. One night, while I was still in the beginning stages of working on this anthology, struggling with early drafts, disillusioned by inequities in the publishing industry and the world at large, I was stunned to see a giant white moth lingering outside my balcony door. It stayed there for nearly ten minutes, attracted by the bright lamp next to my desk, which had been gifted by a translator friend living overseas. At the time, I thought that perhaps the moth was carrying a message of encouragement from Dai and the other poets I had been translating. Looking back now, I see myself in the moth as well. Our fragile silken wings flutter as we take flight together, trailing the voices of the past across pages both familar and new, guided only by the warm light of a lantern glimmering in the dark.

---

1   This is line references the "Butterfly Dream" parable by the Daoist philosopher Zhuangzi and to René Descartes's quote "I think, therefore I am."

2   Jin Kemu 金克木 was a Chinese poet, literary scholar, and translator. He was also the Chinese translator of Simon Newcomb's book *Popular Astronomy*.

3   Dai Wangshu 戴望舒, "Shīlùn Língzhā" 诗论零札 (Brief Fragments on Poetic Theory)," in *Dài Wàngshū shīwén* 戴望舒诗文: 雨巷 (Dai Wangshu's Poetry and Essays: Rainy Alley) (Běijīng 北京: Sānchén yǐngkù yīnxiàng chūbǎnshè 三辰影库音像出版社, 2017).

4   Dai Wangshu 戴望舒, "Èzhīhuā duōyīng yìhòujì" 《恶之花》 掇英译后记 ("The Best of *Les Fleurs du mal*" Translator's Afterword), in *Dài Wàngshū yìshījí* 戴望舒译诗集 (The Poetry Translations of Dai Wangshu) ed. Shi Zhecun 施蛰存 (Chángshā 长沙: Húnán rénmíng chūbǎnshè 湖南人民出版社, 1983), 153–54.

5 Shi Zhecun 施蛰存, "Qiányán" 前言 (Preface), in *Dài Wàngshū yìshījí* 戴望舒译诗集 (The Poetry Translations of Dai Wangshu) ed. Shi Zhecun (Chángshā 长沙: Húnán rénmíng chūbǎnshè 湖南人民出版社, 1983), 1.

6 Dai Wangshu 戴望舒, "Hánghǎi rìjì" 航海日记 (Diaries from a Sea Voyage), in *Dài Wàngshū shīwén: yǔxiàng* 戴望舒诗文: 雨巷 (Dai Wangshu's Poetry and Essays: Rainy Alley) (Běijīng 北京: Sānchén yǐngkù yīnxiàng chūbǎnshè 三辰影库音像出版社, 2017).

7 Dai Wangshu 戴望舒, "Xiānggǎng de jiùshūshì" 香港的旧书市 (Used Book Markets in Hong Kong), in *Dài Wàngshū shīwén: yǔxiàng* 戴望舒诗文: 雨巷 (Dai Wangshu's Poetry and Essays: Rainy Alley) (Běijīng 北京: Sānchén yǐngkù yīnxiàng chūbǎnshè 三辰影库音像出版社, 2017).

8 Dai Wangshu 戴望舒, "Bālí de shūtān" 巴黎的书摊 (Book Stalls in Paris), in *Dài Wàngshū shīwén: yǔxiàng* 戴望舒诗文: 雨巷 (Dai Wangshu's Poetry and Essays: Rainy Alley) (Běijīng 北京: Sānchén yǐngkù yīnxiàng chūbǎnshè 三辰影库音像出版社, 2017).

9 Dai Wangshu 戴望舒, "Jì Mǎdélǐ de shūshì" 记马德里的书市 (On the Book Markets in Madrid), in *Dài Wàngshū shīwén: yǔxiàng* 戴望舒诗文: 雨巷 (Dai Wangshu's Poetry and Essays: Rainy Alley) (Běijīng 北京: Sānchén yǐngkù yīnxiàng chūbǎnshè 三辰影库音像出版社, 2017).

10 Dai Wangshu 戴望舒, "Jì shīrén Xǔbàiwéiàiěr" 记诗人许拜维艾尔 (On the Poet Supervielle), in *Dài Wàngshū shīwén: yǔxiàng* 戴望舒诗文: 雨巷 (Dai Wangshu's Poetry and Essays: Rainy Alley) (Běijīng 北京: Sānchén yǐngkù yīnxiàng chūbǎnshè 三辰影库音像出版社, 2017).

11 Hai An 海岸, "Biān hòu jì" 编后记 (Editor's Afterword), in *Zhōngxī shīgē fānyì bǎinián lùnjí* 中西诗歌翻译百年论集 (A Centennial Anthology of Essays on the Translation of Chinese and Western Poetry) (Shànghǎi wàiyǔ jiàoyù chūbǎnshè 上海外语教育出版社, 2007).

12 Dai Wangshu 戴望舒, "Xīhānuò yìwén shāngzhuó" 《西哈诺》 译文商酌 (Discussions on the Translation of *Cyrano*), in *Dài Wàngshū quánjí dìèrjuàn* 戴望舒全集第二卷 (The Complete Works of Dai Wangshu Vol.2) (Chángchūn 长春: Shídài wényì chūbǎnshè 时代文艺出版, 2000).

Notes

As a native speaker of Mandarin who obtained my Chinese literary education in Simplified Chinese, I have decided to use the Simplified script throughout the book, because it is the one that I am most familiar with. All transliterations have been romanized based on the conventions of the Pīnyīn system. I have endeavored to preserve the tone marks whenever Pīnyīn appears. The only exception that I have made is for the names for people, given that tone marks are generally not included when Chinese names are written in English.

Some of Qiu Jin's poems exist in multiple conflicting versions because her work was mostly published posthumously by different editors who compiled her work from scattered publications and handwritten manuscripts. An earlier version of "Púsāmán: To a Female Friend," which first appeared in *Asymptote*, was translated from a different version of the poem by Qiu Jin. Since then, I have identified a longer and more complete version of the poem, which I have used and re-translated for this book. Whenever there are discrepancies among different versions of Qiu Jin's work, I have used the versions recommended by 《秋瑾诗文选注》(人民文学出版社, 2011), edited by Guo Yanli 郭延礼 and Guo Zhen 郭蓁.

Zhang Qiaohui's poems are excerpted from her manuscript 《青鸾舞镜》. When translating Fei Ming's poetry, I used the versions of his work as identified in 《杀像之意:废名的诗》(百花文艺出版社, 2020). Xiao Xi's poems are excerpted from her book 《风不止》(上海文艺出版社, 2019). When translating Dai Wangshu's poetry, I used the versions of his work as identified in 《望舒草》(浙江文艺出版社, 1997).

Acknowledgements 致谢

Thank you to my editors, Khashayar Mohammadi and Chenxin Jiang, for their care, insightful feedback, and probing questions, which have made this book so much better and taught me so much. Thank you to Ciaoyin Luo for painting the perfect cover art and Jasmine Gui for all the lovely typesetting in Chinese and the careful proofreading. Thank you to Sonia Urlando for her help with the copy edits and her attention to detail, especially given the tight deadlines. Thank you so much to the whole team at Invisible Publishing, especially my publisher Norm Nehmetallah, Megan Fildes, Jules Wilson, Mylène Bouilly, and Kimberley Griffiths, for believing in this project and for helping to make it a reality.

This book would not be possible without the powerful and moving poems of the five Chinese poets whose work I have had the honour of translating. 在此，谨对诗人秋瑾，废名，戴望舒，小西和张巧慧表达最深的敬意。能够与小西老师和张老师合作是我的荣幸，非常感谢您们。

Thank you to the editors and staff at the following publications, where earlier versions of my translations have appeared: *POETRY, Guernica, Room, The Common, Samovar, The Ex-Puritan, LA Review of Books'* "China Channel," *Prism International,* and *Asymptote.* I'm very grateful to the American Literary Translators Association's Virtual Travel Fellowship program and to the Access Copyright Foundation's Marian Hebb Research Grant for supporting my work translating Qiu Jin's poetry. Thank you to everyone who has supported me during the copyright incident with the British Museum; I would not have been able to find the strength to fight such a large institution without your words of encouragement, donations, and organizing efforts.

Thank you to Professor Thomas DeZauche for generously sharing his knowledge of Buddhism with me. Thank you to Professor Gregory Lee and Alba Lorena Barrera for helping me to access Dai Wangshu's non-fiction writings. I truly appreciate Linseng 蓮, Shih-Shin Lee 李世馨, and Catherine for their help cross-checking my understanding of the source texts, including the many idioms, allusions, and cultural references. If there are any mistakes in explaining any allusions, context, or cultural knowledge, the mistakes are mine alone.

Thank you to Gigi Chang for her mentorship, knowledge of Chinese literature, and tips on translation, and to Larissa Lai for her encouragement and wisdom. I am deeply indebted to my friends who have urged me to pursue this project and offered their insightful feedback: Zhui Ning Chang 曾睿宁, yjtc 昀洁, Emily Pate, Judy I. Lin 林怡君, Shyamala Parthasarathy, Nailah King, Hal Y. Zhang, May Huang, Christina Ng, Jane Shi, Haricha Abdaal, Annick MacAskill, Tamara Jong, Kimberley Chong Ling Zhen, and Moira A. Moran. Their time, generosity, and suggestions are so appreciated.

Some of the communities that have sustained me throughout the past three years as I worked on this project are: the Jianghu discord space, the Wandering Sparrows Translators Collective 译派湖燕, the BIPOC Literary Translators Caucus, and the Clarion West Writers Workshop class of 2021.

I would not be where I am today without the support and encouragement of my sworn sister, Léa Taranto, with whom I am always navigating the ups and downs of life. Sending love and hugs, jiějie. Thank you for everything.

About the Poets

Qiu Jin 秋瑾 (1875–1907) was a Chinese writer, poet, essayist, revolutionary, and the founder of the feminist publication *China Women's News* 《中国女报》. Defying the gender expectations of her time, she practised cross-dressing, learned sword-fighting and horseback riding, and acquired a traditional scholarly education. Later, she connected with other activists of China's feminist movement, studied abroad in Japan, and returned home to join a revolution to overthrow the oppressive imperial Qīng dynasty government and fight for women's rights. When the uprising failed, she chose to die as a martyr rather than escape, which led her to become known as a feminist revolutionary icon in China and internationally. In her brief thirty-one years of life before her execution, Qiu Jin wrote over two hundred poems, which have been compiled into various collections posthumously.

Zhang Qiaohui 张巧慧 (1978–) is a Chinese writer, poet, essayist, member of the Chinese Writers Association, and the curator of Chen Zhifo Art Gallery. She has published five poetry collections and an essay collection in Chinese. Her writing has appeared in numerous literary journals, including *People's Literature*, *Poetry Journal*, and *October*, and has been selected for "year's best" anthologies. She has received honors such as the Sanmao Literary Essay Prize. In 2018, *Poetry Journal* named her one of China's "top 20 most innovative women poets."

Fei Ming 废名 (1901–1967) was an influential modern Chinese poet, short story writer, novelist, and essayist, and a member of the Yǔ Sī Sè 语丝社, a literary group founded by Lu Xun 鲁迅 and Zhou Zuoren 周作人. He was the author of various poetry books, short story collections, and novels, including *Mirror* 《镜》, *The*

Stories of the Bamboo Grove《竹林的故事》, and *Bridge*《桥》. Fei Ming's work was deeply influenced by Buddhism, Daoism, and different schools of Chinese philosophy.

Xiao Xi 小西 (1974–) is a poet based in Qīngdǎo in Shāndōng, China. She is the author of two poetry books in Chinese, *Blue Salt* 《蓝色的盐》 and *The Ceaseless Wind*《风不止》. Her poetry has appeared in dozens of Chinese literary publications such as *People's Literature*, *Poetry Journal*, and *October*, and has been published in English translation in *POETRY* and *Guernica*.

Dai Wangshu 戴望舒 (1905–1950) was a poet, editor, translator, and leading figure in the Chinese modernist literature movement. His books include *My Memories*《我底记忆》 and *Troubled Times*《灾难的岁月》. With an interest and education in French literature, he was influenced by the work of French poets such as Paul Fort and Francis Jammes, as well as by ancient Daoist texts and Táng dynasty verse. His writing blends archaic allusions and diction with modern poetics to explore themes such as love, death, and nostalgia.

About the Translator

Yilin Wang 王艺霖 (she/they) is a writer, poet, and Chinese-English translator. Her writing has appeared in *Clarkesworld, Fantasy Magazine, The Malahat Review, Grain, CV2, The Ex-Puritan, The Toronto Star, The Tyee, Words Without Borders,* and elsewhere. She is the editor and translator of *The Lantern and Night Moths* (Invisible Publishing, 2024). Her translations have also appeared in *POETRY, Guernica, Room, Asymptote, Samovar, The Common, LA Review of Books'* "China Channel," and the anthology *The Way Spring Arrives and Other Stories* (TorDotCom, 2022). She has won the Foster Poetry Prize, has received an Honourable Mention in the poetry category of Canada's National Magazine Award, has been longlisted for the CBC Poetry Prize, and has been a finalist for an Aurora Award. Yilin has an MFA in Creative Writing from UBC and is a graduate of the 2021 Clarion West Writers Workshop.

INVISIBLE PUBLISHING produces fine Canadian literature for those who enjoy such things. As an independent, not-for-profit publisher, we work to build communities that sustain and encourage engaging, literary, and current writing.

Invisible Publishing has been in operation for over a decade. We released our first fiction titles in the spring of 2007, and our catalogue has come to include works of graphic fiction and nonfiction, pop culture biographies, experimental poetry, and prose.

We are committed to publishing diverse voices and experiences. In acknowledging historical and systemic barriers, and the limits of our existing catalogue, we strongly encourage writers from LGBTQ2SIA+ communities, Indigenous writers, and writers of colour to submit their work.

Invisible Publishing is also home to the Bibliophonic series of music books and the Throwback series of CanLit reissues.

If you'd like to know more, please get in touch:
info@invisiblepublishing.com

Invisible